Go Compère

A performer's guide to being a compère

By
Wayne Goodman

Go Compere

Copyright © 2019 Wayne Goodman Entertainments.
All rights reserved

No part of this book shall be reproduced or transmitted in any form or by any means, electronic or mechanical, including photocopying, recording, or by any information retrieval system without written permission of the author.

Published by Wayne Goodman Entertainments.
For more copies of this book please email:
wayne@waynegoodman.co.uk
Tel: (+44) 07726 190078
Designed and Set by Wayne Goodman Entertainments

www.waynegoodman.co.uk

ISBN:978-0-9928201-3-8

Cover Art by Michael Murray
Edited by Johnny Toro

Although every precaution has been taken in the preparation of this book, the publisher and author assume no responsibility for errors or omissions. Neither is any liability assumed for damages resulting from the use of this information contained herein.

CAN'T AFFORD THIS BOOK?
A percentage of every book sold subsidises another for those who cannot afford a copy. If you genuinely cannot afford this book & would like to apply for a subsidised copy please contact wayne@waynegoodman.co.uk

This book is dedicated to my beautiful daughter
Charlee Autumn Mae Goodman
My inspiration

Kerrie for joining me on my path.

Ellie, Elise and Celsie

This book would not have been possible without the help of:

My Mum for supporting me all these years through thick and thin.

Richard Whymark

Stacy Smith

Brian Watson.

Daniel & David Bean

The Members of the Ipswich Magical Society.

Special Thanks to Simon Shaw.

Sheriton Swan.
One of the best techies I have ever had the
pleasure to work with.

Rodney James Piper who taught me more than anyone else and showed me how to love the microphone.

Contents

Dedications	2
Contents	3
Forward	5
Introduction	6

Phase One
Before The Show

The Compere	9
The Golden Rules	12
Research - Research - Research	18
Know The Event	23
The Backstage Team	25
Planning The Show	31
Know The Acts	35
Safety First	38

Phase Two
The Show

Opening The Show	**41**
You Are The Compere	**47**
Go Compere	**55**
The Tools At Your Disposal	**61**
The Headliner	**68**
Closing The Show	**70**

To Close

A Chat With Sheriton Swan	**73**
Acknowledgements	**76**
Glossary Of Terms	**77**
Wayne Goodman Page	**80**

Foreword

"Please welcome our compere for the evening".

This is a familiar introduction I have heard many times .

But what makes a good compere?
What is his/her job role?
What qualities do they need?

These and many more questions are answered in this brand new publication by Wayne Goodman.

I have known Wayne as a personal friend for over 20 years and have often sought his advice and opinion on many aspects of the entertainment business.

A good compere can be highly sought after for a show or event as they become the essential link between audience and performer.

Enjoy Waynes experience and advice within these pages and you will gain the valuable knowledge to become a first class compere.

Richard Whymark.

Introduction

This book started when I made an social media post stating that I had no new projects and a close friend Simon Shaw, suggested I do a book on being a compere.

For many years I have been the compere for many different kinds of shows and events.

I have made every mistake possible when it comes to being a compere, I have introduced the wrong act at the wrong time and forgotten acts names but each time I have made a mistake I have learnt from it.

This book is the result of those lessons.

I got into magic when I was 12 years old, but my real education on being an entertainer was in 1995 when I was working in Benidorm, Spain. I was sent there with no knowledge of what I was meant to be doing and soon found myself over my head and out of my depth.

I was a good magician, but I did not like the microphone, had never called Bingo, done a party dance or hosted a quiz.

I somehow managed to survive two or three weeks when I was informed I had another entertainer who was going to be my flatmate.

Rodney James Piper arrived with two bin bags, one full of clothes and one full of playing cards, both got tipped onto the apartment floor and were barely touched for the next 6 months.

Rodney was eccentric and loud and within five minutes of arriving was my best mate.

Rodney took me into Benidorm town for some Alioli and bread and a beer and we discussed magic and what we both did.

When I told him I did not like using the microphone and all the rest, he told me that he would show me how to make the microphone my greatest tool.

I do not know how well my career would have gone if not for the lessons I learnt that winter.

In recent years I have been compere for magic conventions, hosted magic club dinner shows, hosted magic convention lecture shows, been a Bingo caller, quiz master and entertainment coordinator.

It does not matter if you are a magician, a comedian, a Bingo caller, a public speaker, a host, compere or DJ there is something in this book for you, even if it is to learn not to make the same mistakes I did.

I still make mistakes, normally when I do not follow my own advice, and I am still learning. I truly believe every time you walk on stage, every time you pick up a microphone, and everytime you talk to an audience you are learning.

I am lucky to have some amazing friends in the business, and a lot of comments I get from people about my writing style is that reading my books is like having a conversation with me, albeit a one way conversation so please feel free to email me any questions to wayne@waynegoodman.co.uk or contact me through my facebook page.

Thank you for purchasing and reading this book and for the continued support.

Wayne Goodman

PHASE ONE

BEFORE THE SHOW

The Compere

Compere

noun
1. a person who introduces the performers or contestants in a variety show.

verb
1. act as a compère for (a variety show).
2. "Wayne Goodman compèred the whole proceedings"

A Compere is also known as a M.C. or Master of Ceremonies.
Some comperes are referred to as the emcee or host and is the person in charge of running the order of the event.

This could be a wedding, a conference, a party or a specific event like an auction or boxing match.

The compere is there to prepare the crowd, to warm them up, to inform them of the rules of the night and to create atmosphere and to make sure the acts come on to a room that is ready for them.

The compare needs to be prepared for any disruption or delay, and to hold the show together between acts.

No show ever runs smoothly, there are so many moving parts in a show that anything can happen at any time, so the job of the compere is to ensure that no matter what happens, the show carries on.

Your entrance:
The room has slowly filled and the crowd is restless, they are ready for the event and are waiting for the show to start.

You have to make an effective entrance to set a high level for the event. If the compere comes out dull and low then this could easily cause the event to fail. A bad compere will not bring on the acts / speakers etc in a good way and this will destroy the event.

Look at the way sporting events open, like a boxing match or the olympics, it is dramatic and extravagant and it lets you know you are about to see something worth seeing.

Running a show of any kind is a big responsibility and the pressure is on the compere to make sure the energy levels stay high. The atmosphere is like a line on a graph, you want it to go up, not down.

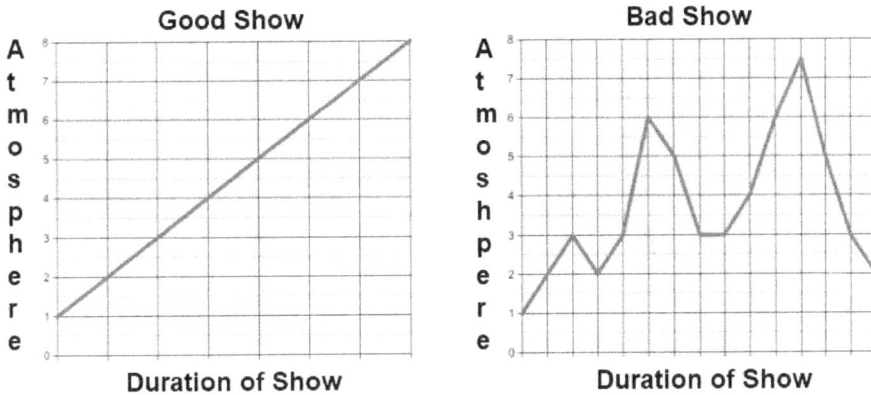

The graph on the left shows how a good show or event should run, with atmosphere building all the way through the acts to the grand finale and the atmosphere peaking.

The graph on the right shows a bad show, with atmosphere going up and down and never really peaking. The graph on the right also has the show ending very low.

The compere has to build the atmosphere from the very start of the show, this means that if the energy of the introduction is low, the energy of the audience will be low and the the act will suffer and struggle to do what they are there to do.

This does not mean you should shout and scream at the audience and jump around etc, the compere has to find the balance and maintain it for the duration of the show.

If you get the energy correct and control the balance then the atmosphere will go up throughout the event and you will be hailed as a great compere.

The Golden Rules

Golden Rule No.1

Do not diminish expectations.

How many times have you seen a show or a presentation and the first thing the compere / emcee / host say's is:

"Be nice, I have never done this before".
"Bear with me, it is my first time".
"I am so nervous".

Would these comments inspire confidence or make you feel excited about the upcoming show?

An unprepared and anxious compere will try to diminish the judgement of the audience before the show has even begun.
This kind of introduction is not only unprofessional but also a little insulting to the audience.

The show has been promoted, the tickets sold and the audience has turned up. The crowd is excited, the show is about to begin.
The compere is introduced and expectations are high and then the compere comes out on stage and kills it with their first words.

You need to have confidence in what you are doing, instead of walking on and playing for sympathy. You are in charge and with that comes the responsibility of making sure the audience have a good time, as well as the responsibility of making sure the acts are brought on in the correct way.

Golden Rule No.2

Do not start the show with a joke.

I remember when I was first asked to compere an event, the first thing I did when I walked out was to tell a great one liner.

It was one that I had used many times in my comedy magic show and it killed every time, and it killed this time too, except it killed the start of the show.

Starting a show or event as an emcee with a joke is never a good idea and for a number of reasons:

- The audience will see it as a needy call for help.
- The joke is out of place or out of context so falls flat with the audience.
- The audience do not know you yet, or your humour.

There are exceptions to the case, I remember seeing a great compere Tony Stevens at the Blackpool Magic Convention, it was the same year that David Blaine performed his stunt in London where he survived in a glass box without food for a prolonged period of time.

Before the show began there was an awards ceremony for the competitions etc which lasted around 30-40 minutes, then the compere was introduced but did not arrive on stage.

It was at this point the table cloth covering the awards table was taken away to reveal there was no table, instead was a glass box with the compere Tony inside.

This great gag brought the house down and was a great start to the show, but it was in context to the show and the audience (who were 99% magicians).

The audience wants to meet YOU and get to know YOU. You are are the host of the show so be courteous and honest and welcoming and if you want to use comedy then introduce it properly as part of your personality and not as a gimmick.

Use the talents you have, if you are funny then great but remember scripted lines and stock jokes do not guarantee a great performance. A good compere is one who embraces comedy without forcing it.

If you are not a funny person then use that, be creative but also be yourself, this will win over the audience much quicker and you can relax and enjoy the experience.

Not every compere has to be funny or a comedian, but the compere does need to be engaging and entertaining.

Golden Rule No.3

Be yourself.

Being yourself on stage is the key to any presentation or performance.

If the audience like you then they will relax and enjoy the show,
If the audience do not like you they will not relax, they will get bored and you will see the pockets of light around the room as they get their phones out or worse, you will see people leaving.

The worst compere's are the ones who do not realise they are not the stars of the show, they think it is all about them.

I have seen compere's who have tried to outdo and upstage the acts and it never bodes well.

I have also seen compere's who are condescending and fake, but the audience is not stupid they will know if you are being fake with them, so be honest and be yourself.

I once saw a ringmaster at a circus show who was so condescending in their presentations that it was almost difficult to watch by the end of the show. This was a real shame though as the ringmaster was confident and more than competent, but their presentation failed because of the way they presented themselves.

In contrast, the ringmaster the following year was amazing and held the audience in the palm of their hand. The main reason for this was because their presentation was the polar opposite of the previous ringmaster. They used their own personality and bonded with the audience instead of alienating themselves from them.

Golden Rule No.4

Expect the unexpected.

It is very rare for a show to run EXACTLY as planned.

Things can change in a matter of seconds and you need to be prepared for it.

- In the past I have had acts who (at the very last minute) have cancelled or changed what they were doing in the show.

- I have had acts who have fallen ill between rehearsal and the start time of the show and with no other acts around to replace them, I have had to do something to fill the time.

- I was on stage in Cancun, Mexico during a hurricane.
  The hotel was being battered and the roof was being ripped off directly above the stage.

  I performed the show using a battery powered karaoke speaker and with two Mexican waiters shining power torches on me to keep me lit. All this happening while my boss stood at the side of the stage, thumbs up telling me it was going great.

There are many kinds of interruptions that can happen during a show, and they come from every direction.

We cannot stop this from happening, it is the nature of live entertainment. Things happen, things go wrong and as compere you are the one who the audience will look at to find out how you will deal with it.

Remember, it is how you deal with it, that defines you as a compere.
For example, this is a story that happened to me a few years back, the whole incident lasted no longer than 20 seconds.

I was compere for a magic convention when an issue with the power for the lights to the stage caused a blackout, the house lights instantly came on but I was on stage with no lights.

I could have panicked or shouted at the lighting techs (which I have seen happen in the past), but instead, I smiled, I kept my composure and I carried on.

The audience looked at me, smiled again and as I looked at them I said,

"Does anyone have £1 for the electricity metre"

It got the laugh I hoped for and a few seconds later the power was back on and everyone applauded.

I maintained composure and control and the problem was dealt with.
If the power had remained off for longer, I would have covered the time, but it was the initial moment that showed everyone I was in control and they were in safe hands.

Be prepared for a fire alarm, be prepared for a disturbance. If you are prepared and they happen, then you are in a better place to deal with it.

Chapter One

Research - Research - Research

When I was 12 years old I was in the Sea Cadets. I loved the sailing and canoeing and trips with the Royal Navy and I was fortunate enough during my time to learn many life lessons. Foremost of these has to be the 6 P's.

Proper Planning Prevents Piss Poor Performance

In every job, task or project the world over the only thing that is certain is that the more research and preparation you have, the better the chance of success.

As a magician a lot of my preparation comes in the form of practice, rehearsal and trial performances. However as a compere in addition to this, I also need as much information about the event as I can get and be able to coordinate before and during the event with the organisers.

To highlight how important research and preparation is I would like to share two stories that I witnessed.

In 2016 I was booked to perform close up magic for a corporate event at the NEC in Birmingham, England. I was invited to stay and watch the show if I would like and I said I may watch a few minutes before heading off. I am so glad I stayed.

The event was a business event run by a number of high level scientists, I had a blast doing magic for them at the tables, (I love performing to scientists, they are so analytical) and then took a seat right at the back to watch a little of the show.

The compere arrived five minutes before the show was supposed to start and was chatting to the events coordinator about 20 yards from where I was sat.

The coordinator gave the compere a running order and was trying to emphasise a couple of points about key moments but the compere just kept saying he had it all in hand and had received an email with all the relevant info on and he knew what he was doing.

What happened next was no surprise and ten minutes later we all knew that his story of preparation was a lie.

Over a very short time the compere managed to turn a so far very successful event into a full on train wreck.

I was furiously writing notes on my phone but some of the highlights were

The compere walked on stage and welcomed everyone to the wrong event. He still had a running order in his pocket from another event and brought out the wrong piece of paper.

Asked the audience how many speakers were on the line up.

The events organiser was called Kathy and the compere kept referring to her as Carol, even after being corrected more than once.

Had to ask for the names of the speakers and award presenters, again all this info was on the running order, in his pocket.

The compere was booked to present some awards, but due to not preparing and not listening to the coordinator, he had trouble saying a couple of names, the names in question were Janson (a Danish name pronounced Yanson) and Adebayo (a Nigerian name) neither name is difficult to pronounce if prepared, instead it turned into a shambles and an embarrassment not only for the event but the awardees themselves.

Because the compere had not read the running order, he closed his part of the event without doing two parts of the presentation, meaning he had to be called back up onto the stage to finish his part. The compere decided to break the absolute biggest rule of being a compere and publicly blamed the organisation for not giving him the right information.

Speaking with the coordinator afterwards, she told me, no one had sent him an email (she had checked whilst he was on) and the correct and complete running order was still in his pocket.

Now let's get straight to the point and say that this was a terrible compere. If he had been even slightly prepared then none of the above would have happened. I have seen worse comperes, but he is definitely in my top five worst emcee's.

I know or have known some of the most amazing compere's in the business, I have also seen or worked under some of the worst compere's ever to take to the stage and almost every time the difference comes down to preparation.

I was at a wedding a few years ago and the Groom had two best men, both were his brothers, one was an entertainer and one a computer programmer.

The father of the bride gave his speech and was well accepted, it was moving and from the heart and well written.

The Groom gave his speech and went down well too, he glowed as he praised his wife, his family and everyone at the wedding, again well thought out and honest.

The first best man, the computer programmer, gave a funny speech full of prepared stories that, whilst mildly embarrassing for the groom, gave an insightful look into the relationship between the brothers.

The second brother, who is an entertainer, thought he could wing it, had no speech prepared and rambled on for over 30 minutes.

He could have or should have prepared a speech, at the very least he could have coordinated with his brother and shared some stories so they would both compliment each other.

Instead, through over confidence or arrogance he trampled on the other speakers, made a total embarrassment of himself and brought the atmosphere of the whole event to a standstill.

The simple solution to both these scenarios is prior research and preparation.

So what do you need to know from the client?
Well the simple truth is, I could fill a book with just questions you need to ask a client, however every show, presentation, award ceremony and every seminar is different and requires its own set of questions.

You need to look at the event and then decide what do you need to know about the event to make it a success.

The simple way to get all the answers you want is to arrange to meet with the coordinator for a full consultation on the requirements they have and also the role you will be playing in the show.

A few simple questions to start you off should be:

- Audience size and demographic
- Tone – what is the appropriate / preferred feel of the event
- Language – are there any restricted words or sensitivities?
- Venue details
- Detailed running order
- Key messaging – what does the company hope to convey?
- Script
- Will the attendee's be eating before or during the show?
- How big is the room in the venue?
- How long should the show last?
- How scripted do you want the show to be?
- How many speakers / acts / awards etc to be presented?
- Full list of names and information for all speakers / acts etc.
- Who is the headline act / speaker?
- What are the emergency procedures for the event?

Think about the information you need to make the show work.

Try to think one step ahead of every question you ask, for example if they want an hour show then plan for an hour and a half.

I want to finish this section with a couple of quick quotes.

> *"If you fail to prepare, then you can prepare to fail"*
>
> Benjamin Franklin

There is an another classic saying;

> *"Knowing is half the battle"*
>
> G.I. Joe

Who knew G.I. Joe was so full of wisdom?
The quote stands though and knowing who they are, what is happening and why they are there, is half the battle won.

Chapter Two

Know the event.

Knowing the event is the most important part of being a compere, and to know the event means you, as the compere, need to have as much information as you can. This leads you to the three W's.

Who? - What? - Why?

Who are the audience?
What is happening at the event?
Why are they at the event?

The first question when preparing to be a compere is to ask who am I performing to:

- Adults
- Families
- Children
- Organised groups
- Professional groups

Does the group consist of only adults?
If yes, what kind of performance are they expecting?
Remember a military audience is a world away from a Women's Institute show in regards to what they are expecting.

If the audience is families or children, what are the ages of the children? Are you prepared and equipped to entertain this age group? Will the children be sat with the adults or on their own?

Each question you ask the client, when answered should open up more questions.

Now you know who you are performing for, you need to know what is happening and why they are there.

- Corporate (conference, seminar)
- Family event or party.
- Organisation (WI - company - Speciality group like a magician's group)
- Sporting event (boxing, soccer etc)
- Wedding or anniversary event.
- Awards ceremony

Once you know what kind of event you will be hosting you can start working on a running order and plan for the event.

Do not be scared to ask questions of the client, they will be happy to answer and it shows you know what you are doing.

That being said, do not pester the client constantly with questions. I have heard stories of compere's sending five or ten emails a day with singular or a couple of questions.

A much better way is to sit down and work out what you need to know and then send one email or arrange a consultation either in person
or telephone / skype etc.
Get all the answers at one time, or two if a follow up is required.

Ask the questions, get the answers and you are one step closer to being fully prepared for the show.

Chapter Three

The Backstage Team

Even when you work alone, when you are in a show, or presenting a seminar, you are part of a bigger team.

Backstage Team:
During the show the only people behind the curtain or in the wings should be those that need to be there.

Other acts should be set and in the green room, ready to come out when required, and only the compere and any required backstage crew should be anywhere near the stage.

Make sure the backstage crew know who is needed and at what time, you do not want to be rushing off to find crew members or trying to coordinate them during the show.

The Stage Technicians:
Before the event starts, before any attendee's or audience is allowed in the room, you should be talking to and coordinating with the sound and lights team.

It is not always possible to have a full run through, so at the very least you should be doing:

- Sound check
- Light check
- Running order check

When I am hosting a show, I will get to the venue very early, normally I am the first one there. This way I can look at the empty venue and visualise what is about to happen there.

I love the sounds and atmosphere of an empty theatre that is building up to a show that evening. I will do a sound check and make sure I sound clear and crisp, and that I can be heard in every corner of the room.

I will also wander around the performance area to ensure I know where any problem or dropout zones are, these are places the microphone cuts out or the sound dips.

In the last few years the technology of wireless microphones has improved in leaps and bounds but in some venues and in some spaces they can still cut out or lose the signal.

If like me, you like to wander around as you work, and talk to people in the audience, then you need to know where you can and can not go.

I will do a lighting check too, I want to know that the audience can see me, and can see what is about to happen on the whole stage.

A lighting check also allows for me to make sure I can see too, I need to be able to see the stage, the oncoming / offgoing acts, the route off stage and also I may need to read notes whilst on stage. I do not want to be blinded because I did not check the lights before hand nor do I want to be left in the dark, both literally and metaphorically.

I will also, whilst on the microphone, do a full run through of all the acts and their introductions. I want to make sure I get all the names correct, I know all the information about the acts, and I know where I need to be to do the introduction.

Cues:
A cue is a message to the compere or act on stage. Most cues to the stage are sent using the lights. Some lighting cues can be public like a flashing side light or spotlight, and some can be more discreet like a specific cue light.

A cue light is a small light that only the person on stage can see.

Venue cue systems come in many different shapes and sizes, some are a stand alone unit like the image below, some are lights that are built into the stage or surrounding area.

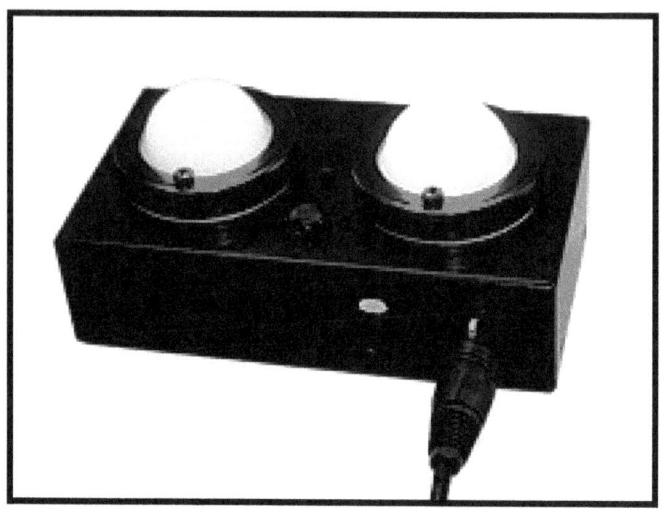

The unit is constructed with two small lights.

Most units use a red and green system but you may find other units that use different colours but the procedure is still the same, for the sake of this example we will continue with the normal system of a red/green lighting system.

The cue system is basically a traffic light system for the compere.

The red light means **STOP**, do not introduce the next act.

The green light means **GO**, the next act is ready.

The cue light will be red when the act is setting up behind the curtain or off stage and then will turn green when the act is ready to be introduced.

The basic meaning of the red light is for the compere to keep talking, keep the show moving until the green light comes on.

Being prepared for the delay (by coordinating with the acts, more on this later) means you have an approximate time to fill, the lighting cue just confirms that the act is ready and you can introduce the act and keep the show on track.

Coordinate with the light and sound engineers
I always make a point of knowing and respecting the engineers behind the light and sound desk.

The engineers behind the desk are the real wizards and a little time spent with them beforehand, and a public thank you whilst on stage goes a long way.

In every show I do, I try and have a small joke with the light and sound engineers. Something as simple as asking for the lights to be dipped or brightened, when it does not happen I berate the engineers and all the lights are turned off, this gets a laugh with the audience and then they come back on.

This may sound very simple and an easy laugh, which it is, but do not underestimate the power of using simplicity.

This little joke introduces the audience to the light and sound techs, it brings them into the show. They are a major, yet unseen, part of the performance and allowing them to win the (fake) situation and get the laugh will mean a lot to them, and it shows they have a sense of humour.

I love any interaction with the off stage staff and will go into more details about this later in the book.

It is always worth speaking to the backstage crew when you arrive back at the theatre or venue before the show starts to make sure that there have been no major changes to the show or event.

I should state that during this story, I was not the compere, merely an act in a much bigger show, but it is still worth keeping up to date on any changes in the show.

I was working on a huge stage for a large show back in the late 1990's, my part of the show was simple, I was to walk to the centre of the stage and perform a magic trick with a newspaper. The problem was I was to do this in pitch blackness with a single spotlight on me.

Not having any idea where on the stage I was going to end up, I decided to do a run through in the afternoon.

I measured from the curtains to a point just forward of the centre of the stage, it was approximately eight of my normal steps.

That evening, I was backstage and on my cue I walked to the curtains and waited for them to open, this would be my moment to walk the planned 8 steps and present my effect.

The compere announced me, the music started and the curtains opened. I stepped out into total darkness except for the blinding light in my eyes, I smiled and walked forward, another step, and another, I was walking in a brisk manner towards my planned mark on the stage and as I took my fifth step I suddenly vanished from the stage … gone.

The sound and light technicians, confused brought up the side lights and sure enough the stage was completely empty, I had vanished and the audience went wild.

So what happened? Where had I gone? How had I done it?

Well the answer was simple, and even now, a little painful.
Between my measuring the stage at 2pm and leaving to come back later, the show producers changed the lineup for the show, which now included a bigger illusion act for the headline spot.

This meant more space was needed backstage so the curtains were moved approx 8 feet forward. This was no big deal to the theatre as the curtains had 3 different rails they could fit on due to the number of shows they had and the different requirements of these shows.

So when I walked through the curtains I was unaware of the change in the size of the front of curtains / stage area. I was walking my 8 steps to get me to the spot I had determined was a good spot and unbeknown to me, I was actually walking off the front of the stage into the musicians pit, which was luckily empty.

As I lay in the darkness like a dropped lasagne, in quite a bit of pain, my groans of agony were drowned out by the applause of the audience who had just witnessed a miracle.

Chapter Four

Planning the show.

The show is booked, the acts are booked, you get the running order and coordinate with the organisers so you know all the important details and you have made arrangements for a rehearsal and sound and lighting check.

So what else is there to do before the event for you as the compere?

Well quite a lot actually and the first thing to do is make a show plan.

The show plan is basically a running order with a little more information that is directly aimed at what you need to know.

I have included on the next page a copy of a show plan I wrote for a Magic Convention in Harrogate, England in 2014.

As you can see, all my moments are highlighted so I can see at a glance what I need to cover and how long I need to do.

By coordinating with the show producer and with some forward thinking we were quickly able to put together a running order that would compliment each act, and allow a smooth changeover of acts.

- Music for audience entrance.
- **My introduction.**
- First act - Illusion act, act length 12 minutes.
- **1st bridge - ninety seconds required.**
- Second act - Traditional Magic, act length 8 minutes.
- **2nd bridge - 3 minutes required.**
- Third act - Comedy Magic act, act length 12 minutes.
- **Close first half.**

- - Interval - 20 mins

- **Open second half.**
- First Act - Juggling act, act length 8 minutes.
- **3rd bridge, ninety seconds required.**
- First Headliner, Comedy magic act, act length 15 minutes - 1 false tab.
- **4th bridge, four minutes required.**
- Second Headliner, Illusion act, act length 15 minutes - 1 false tab.
- **Recall all acts for close.**
- **Close second half.**

The changing of the acts:
Different acts require different times to set up, and in this case we only had a few acts, so the backstage team did not have too much pressure when it came to changing the acts. This will not always be the case.

The first act was an illusion act, they had all the time before the show to set up on stage so no pressure there.

The second act needed 90 seconds to get there table and box on stage after the curtain closed. The second act was a traditional magic act, this was done in front of the curtains.

This meant there was a window of 12 ½ minutes covering the first bridge, second performance, and the second bridge for the first act to clear their set and the third act to prepare theirs.

The changing of the act should have taken less than 10 minutes. However to ensure all was good behind the curtain I prepared for a 3 minute bridge.

Even if it was not needed I was prepared to cover for this time.

The third act, which had minimal setup was ready to go within this time scale and was able to relax backstage for a few minutes before being introduced.

The second half ran smoothly with the only problem being that both headline acts wanted to work with open curtains.

This meant the last act, which requires big stage props etc, had to set up between the first headliner and their own spot. This required a longer bridge, which meant I had to cover a longer time, to allow the illusion act to set behind the curtain, (4th bridge, 4 minutes).

This was problematic as I am the compere, I am not there to compete with the acts, I am there to compliment them, but I am also a comedy magician. I cannot go on stage after a headline comedy magician and do more comedy magic. Therefore I had to rethink my performance and make sure this spot not only kept the show moving at the right pace, but also was not seen to upstage the previous (headliner) act.

If you look at the plan above you will see I needed to cover four minutes. Four minutes does not seem a long time to cover, but it can be an eternity when you are on stage, alone and outside your comfort zone.

Luckily, and because I was prepared, I was able to cover this time easily with a couple of well chosen gags and some compere cheats:

- I called for applause for all the previous acts.
- I congratulated and thanked the organisers.
- I gave a quick bio of the last act and built anticipation for what the audience was about to see.

Sounds simple and easy, and it is, but without planning and prep, this would have been a slow moment in the show and had a negative impact on the big finale.

Bridging:
One word that is repeated a few times above is "Bridge".
This is not a card game, bridging is the term used for the time between acts, when you as the compere need to bridge the space and fill the dead time, so the show does not slow down or stop.

Bridging time is mainly determined by the amount of time the leaving act and the oncoming act requires to be ready. You need to speak with every act and determine their requirements, so you know what you need to prepare and how long you need to do to cover this time.

When I am planning my bridging time, I will always double what is expected as well as having other pieces planned.

So if an act tells me they need two minutes I plan for four. This preparation means I will not be caught short and have to try and wing any extra time required due to an unseen complication.

Chapter Five

Know the acts.

A good compere is one who creates a bond with acts they are about to introduce. I have one simple rule when it comes to hosting a show:

"I will not introduce strangers in the show".

In other words I want to meet and know the acts before I introduce them. I will always meet the acts before the show, even if it is just for five minutes when they arrive at the venue.

A very quick meet and greet to make sure I have all the correct info puts us both at ease and allows for a better interaction on stage.

It is not just about how they want to be introduced, it is also about how they do NOT want to be introduced. Some acts have met horrendous comperes who butcher the show for their own ego's, belittle acts and alienate the audience. So do not be surprised if an act arrives with a list of demands about how they will not be brought on stage.

Normally a quick five minute chat will put them at ease that I am not that kind of compere, and break down a few anxiety barriers about how the show is going to run and be run that evening.

For most of my shows I use a compere sheet, this single page tells me everything I need to know about the act and how to prepare my spots in the show.

Below is an image of a simple compere sheet and it features four main points for me to use.

Wayne Goodman Compere Sheet.

Compere Sheet:

Name of act:

Duration:

Last Item in show:

False Tab:

The name of the act.
The name of the act refers to how the act wants to be introduced.
You may know the act as Michael and Tamsyn but on stage and to the audience they are known as High Jinx.

The space for the name is large enough you can make some notes if the act has any requirements on their introduction, such as warnings of pyrotechnics, flashing lights etc.

The duration of the act.
Knowing the length of the act is essential when it comes to planning the run and flow of the show.

The last item in show.
I am always aware of the last piece the act will perform this way I can ensure I am in the wings ready to walk on and / or bring off the act.

The worst thing that can happen, and something that I have seen many times, with poor compere's is the act announcing they have finished, getting a round of applause and the compere running on because they were unaware that the act was coming to an end.

Does the act require a false tab?
A false tab is when an act leaves the stage and comes back to do "one more thing". Most acts in a show do not have a false tab with the exception of the headline acts or acts that require it as part of their performance.

Once I have all the information I need I am one step closer to making sure I can do my job and introduce the act to the audience in the best way.

Chapter Six

Safety First.

This will not be the biggest chapter in this book but its place is necessary, I have in 25 years had 2 total evacuations during a show, and from speaking to friends and colleagues in the business that is a high number.
It is rare but it does happen.

The details of both these situations are as follows.

A fire in the kitchen of the restaurant attached to the venue.
This was not a major issue and were back in theatre 20 minutes after the alarms sounded. What was funny here was that we were probably safer in the theatre, (which was nowhere near the restaurant), than we were in the busy road opposite.

A small electrical fire from the sound desk in the venue.
This situation was a little bit more complicated than the last one as it was on board a Mini-Cruise between Finland and Norway, and although I was not the Compere, I was on stage with the microphone when it happened, therefore I was the face of the emergency.

All cruise ships and ferries have regular fire and emergency alarm drills so it was no major issue to get them out of the entertainments lounge to the designated safety spots. This situation was also dealt with quickly and I was able to carry on with my show about 45 minutes after the alarms sounded.

Both situations were dealt with quickly and calmly and as soon as it was done we moved forward and got the event / show back underway.

The main key to success for dealing with situations like these is:

- Remain calm.
- Keep the audience calm.
- Stay in control.
- Constant communication with both the audience and the venue staff.

The host and compere is seen as the one in charge so if the unthinkable happens, you will be seen as the voice of calm and the person who has the answers about what to do next.

By law every venue should have an evacuation plan so ask the staff for a copy, this will detail fire assembly points and all the exits from the venue.

Learn and know these details so that if the unthinkable happens you can remain calm and inform everyone of what is happening and what they need to do.

An alarm will never happen at a good time in the show, but if and when it does happen you need to be prepared for it.

PHASE TWO

THE SHOW

Chapter Seven

Opening the show

Opening the show and your introduction is a big part of the show. This opening will set the tone and level of the show.

If your opening and introduction is weak and low energy it will kill the rest of the night.
If it is strong and high energy it will create a wave that will carry you forward.

The first voice the audience will hear is normally the compere's and it needs to be strong and bold, in control and confident. This is not the time to "umm" or "ahh", it should be short and most importantly prepared in advance.

There are two parts to opening a show, the introduction of the compere and the setting up the rules of the show.

Make an entrance:
Some compere's are happy to just walk out on stage and say "Good evening", however is this enough to make an impactful entrance?

When you walk on stage you are making a statement of being in control and that you are someone who they want to listen to and to respond to.

The Introduction:
A voice over introduction, which is someone introducing you, can be done a number of different ways, you can get someone to introduce you on stage, you can have a pre recorded introduction or you can do it yourself from behind the curtain or offstage.

If you have someone there who is proficient enough to introduce you, then write down what you want them to say and have them practice it a few times before they actually have to do it for the show.

Some people prefer to have a pre recorded professionally made introduction that the sound techs can play to bring you on. There are plenty of places online who will record and send you the MP3 of whatever you want them to say.

Over the last couple of years a lot of acts have paid for the voice of Peter Dickson. Peter Dickson is the voice over man who is best known for the X-Factor and Britains Got Talent. For a premium rate he will record your introduction in his famous voice.

Using a professional voice artiste and a scripted pre-recorded introduction is one way ensure a smooth start to your show.

A lot of compere's like to just do it themselves, from backstage or behind the curtain, they will say the words and make the introduction.

I normally do my own introduction it is short and simple and to the point.

"Ladies and gentlemen".
"Please, put your hands together and welcome to the stage".
"Your host and compere for this evening".
"The one … the only."
"Mr …… Wayne Goodman".

I have a pause of maybe half a second between each line and also put a little emphasis on the first word of each line to raise the anticipation for what they are about to see.

I also have a pre-recorded version of the above and that has some high energy intro music behind it.

I had the original Chicago Bulls Intro Music playing which builds so that when my name is said at the end, it is a natural applause puller.

Another great song is "Let's get ready to rumble" by the Jock Jams, but now I have an original piece of music that a musician friend of mine created. Make sure you have the right licenses and permissions for the music you are going to use.

Using music is a great way to build the atmosphere and let the audience know that something is happening and about to happen.

Sporting events, awards ceremonies and big comedy events all have introduction music for the hosts and it really adds to the dynamic of the occasion.

One industry that really knows how to do an introduction is the WWE or the World Wrestling Entertainment. They really raise the atmosphere in the room and have a build up that has the audience on the edge of their seats, ready to explode.

Wayne and Dr Philip Hammond at a conference at the NEC

Walking out:
With my name called I can now make my entrance. The curtains open, or I walk through them, I am visible and I have one chance to make a good impression and win the crowd.

I walk to the front of the stage, right in the centre, and with my arms outstretched I take a small bow and accept their applause.

The welcoming stance

By stretching my arms out to the sides I am opening myself up to the audience.

This is (in body language terms) called an indicator, it draws people to you. It signals you have a confident, approachable attitude and creates a positive impression.

This position says you have nothing to hide, you are sincere, direct and trustworthy. It puts people at ease with you which is exactly what you want when standing in front of an audience.

Combine this action with a huge smile and small bow and you should make a connection with the audience that will allow you to start the show properly.

First words:
So you are on stage, the audience is applauding and you are in the moment. The first words you say to the audience are as important as the introduction you just received.

As stated before, you do not want to open with a joke, the audience wants to meet you, to see you and hear what you have to say, so open with a statement.

My first words are normally, "Good Evening everyone. Welcome to the show and what a show we have for you this evening".

If it is not a show I may change the last part to, "We have an amazing lineup of speakers for you tonight".

Remember the compere does not have to be funny, and does not want to be funnier than the acts, the compere is not the star of the show.

If you want to use comedy then watch some live comedy shows, when the compere comes on they will never open with a joke, it is always a welcome statement, a pause and then the set up for the first routine or joke.

Setting the tone:
You are on, you have been introduced and the crowd is excited for the show and now you need to set the tone of the show.

The compere is the face of the show, they are seen to be in control and it is up to the compere to control the tone of the show.

There are times to be serious and times to have a laugh, this is more apparent in a business event than a comedy show but it still applies.

If the compere does not control the tone and pace of the show there will be little or no focus from the audience, the acts or speakers will suffer and the event will fail.

Chapter Eight

You are the Compere

The job of the compere is to introduce the acts and keep the show moving. In this chapter I am going to look at a few things you can do that will help you make a connection with the audience.

Smile:
It sounds silly when you talk to people and you mention that smiling is one of the most important things you can do when in the spotlight.

Being a host / emcee can be stressful and nerve wracking, and if it is the first time you have done it, then you are naturally going to be feeling anxious and worried about how the show will go.

But do not underestimate the power of a sincere smile.

Tom Wilson said,

> *"A smile is happiness that you find right under your nose".*

A lot of books on body language will tell you the physical and mental benefits to smiling but for the point of view of being on stage I will share just three.

Chemical Happiness:
When you smile, your body releases endorphins, this is a natural chemical in the human body. This same chemical is released when you work out, in the gym or doing any physical exercise, some people refer to this as a "Runner's High".

You can see the effects of this, when someone heckles a politician, or when something goes wrong on stage, the lead person will smile, and when they smile, everyone relaxes because you know that the person in charge will have the answer.

Releasing endorphins also reduces stress and anxiety, so when you are nervous before the show, as you walk out onto the stage … "Smile" and you will feel those butterflies vanish, you will relax and your presentation / act will flow much better.

Smiling releases positive emotions too, that is why we often feel happier around children, they smile a lot, and then so do you.

Smiling makes you appear trustworthy:
You are about to stand in front of a room of people, maybe strangers, maybe your peers and ask them to watch, listen and maybe learn from you. To do this, whether it is for an act, a presentation or a seminar you have to build trust.

Research has shown that smiling establishes you as a better leader and worthy of trust.

A University of Pittsburgh study revealed people who smile are more approachable, trustworthy and have more likability than people with non smiling facial expressions.

A study at the University of Montpellier, France concluded that smiling is as strong a reflection of leadership qualities as confidence and compassion

Smiling is a gift that spreads:
How many times have you looked at someone and smiled, and they have smiled back? Smiling is like yawning or frowning, it is often referred to as a sign of empathy.

If you see someone frown, you may also find yourself frowning. Everyone knows if you see someone yawn, then get ready for a yawn yourself.

And it appears that smiling is another that is easily spread. When you smile at the audience, they will smile back at you and everyone feels better and more connected.

Remember:

> **"Nothing you wear is more important than your smile".**

Connie Stevens

Make your script a conversation with the audience:
Nobody wants to sit and watch someone reading something verbatim off a piece of paper with a monotonous voice that neither inspires or entertains.

Write your script and learn your script, rehearse it so it sounds natural and then use notes to remind you of the key points, but do not repeat it word for word, instead turn your monologue into a conversation.

When I am on stage, I talk to the audience, I ask questions and I interact with the audience member based on the answers I get.

I do not belittle or berate the audience member, I may have some banter with them for comedic virtue, but I do not turn the audience member into a prop to get laughs on my behalf.

Instead I ask questions and elevate the audience member to a higher status, when I finish the conversation the spectator feels part of the show and not embarrassed or humiliated.

I stick to my script, but allow for a certain degree of deviation for the bridging sections of the show.

Speaking to people after my shows, I get a lot of comments about how they felt they were also part of the show, their contribution was made to be important.

Eye to Eye:
When you are on stage, it is so important to make eye contact with every member of the audience

If you are hosting a small conference with 50 people then this appears easy but if you are on stage in front of 500 people this appears to be a little bit more problematic. Especially as on stage with all the house lights off and stage lights on you can barely see the front row.

Actually in reality and with a little thought you will find that it is no problem to appear to make eye contact with every member of the audience.

Some books tell you to imagine a line across the room and keep looking at that line as well as looking left and right.

This is fine and can be great if you are working in a boardroom or a classroom and you have 20 to 50 people sat in front of you.

However if you are in a large conference room with 200 people or in a theatre with 500 people or 1000 people then this system falls a little flat and just makes it look like your shifting your gaze from one side of the room to the other.

I have a different approach and one that works much better for me and the way I present.

I want the audience, and by that I mean every member of the audience to feel like I am talking directly to them, looking directly at them and engaging with them to the point they feel like they are an actual part of the event / show.

Divide and Engage:
This room is from a theatre, it holds a large number of people sat across different levels.

As you can see from the above, there are various sections to the seating.

I will now break down these different sections and mentally create a pattern, for this next image I have assigned the pattern across the different sections.

This simple method allows me to repeatedly look across different cross sections of the audience which means they will get the feeling you are actually looking at them, making eye contact with them, and they will feel more part of the show.

I have read elsewhere that when looking at a section of theatre to make a connection with the audience you need to look for a minimum of 3 seconds.

You have to remember that this image is much smaller than an actual theatre, even moving from one side to the other will require an actual shifting of the head from one side to the other.

You should also make the transition from each section slow and smooth, it should look like you are just shifting your gaze and not a premeditated action.

When looking at this image, try to imagine you are on the stage, and make the physical action of looking around the room at the different sections in the order of the numbers.

By shifting my gaze and dividing my time with each section I am able to connect with the audience and have them feel like I was looking directly at them, and thus making them feel that they are an actual involved in what I am saying and doing.

I should add here that all of this has become a subconscious action now, I do not need to think about it, I have my pattern and no matter the size or shape of the room, I can apply it to every audience.

Here is a smaller venue, still with tiered seating.

Now let us add the eye contact formula to the smaller venue.

As you can see the formula still works, it maybe a little more condensed but I can still move my vision around the room in the same manner.

Like any other aspect of performing, to make this look natural it will take practice.

Remember:
- Make the actions small and subtle.
- Do not panic if you miss a section, this should be a natural motion not a conscious action.
- Look **into** the spaces, not **at** the spaces.
- Imagine the people smiling at you, and remember to smile back.

Over time you will also be able to do this without having to think about it.

Chapter Nine

Go Compere

So everything has built to this moment, the audience is seated and the lights are dimmed, the audience goes quiet and you walk on stage and do the intro you have prepared. Everything is going great, the audience is responsive and you see the cue light switch to green, the first act is ready.

Introducing the Act:
Depending on the event you are presenting will define the introduction, for instance if the event is a presentation or lecture etc, then you should spend a minute or two to announce some of the presenters credentials or past achievements. This should not be a full bio but just a few highlights to wet the appetite of the audience.

If the event is a show, then you can bypass this and get the act on, maybe a quick sentence if the act would like it such as;

"Our first act is well known to you for his TV appearances".

Or

"This act has just returned from a successful summer cruising the world".

More than this is overkill and will just slow the show down.

Say my name, say my name:
The most important part of being an emcee / compere is introducing the acts or speakers.

Do it right and you will ensure the act is welcomed on stage in the best way. Do it wrong and you could kill the act, and the show.

Name of the act.
One of the worst things you can do is ruin the intro by announcing the name of the act before you introduce them properly.

An example of this is:

"Ladies and Gentleman, up next we have Wayne Goodman".
"Wayne is a comedy magician, who is well known on the comedy circuit".
"So please put your hands together ….. Wayne"

I have been introduced like that a number of times, and it is always an uphill start to make a connection with the audience after that.

For starters the name should be an applause clue, when your name is announced that is the moment the audience should start clapping.

Do not mention the name of the act until the end of the introduction, not only does this mean the applause will all happen at the same time but it helps to build anticipation with the audience.

Let the introduction do all the work and build up the audience ensuring the moment you name the act, the audience will spontaneously start to clap.

The proper way to introduce an act is:

"Ladies and Gentleman, up next we have a regular name on the magic convention circuit".
"Please put your hands together for the amazing comedy magic of".
"Mr ….. Wayne Goodman".

The Entrance:
The act is walking out and the audience is applauding, your job now is to move aside and allow the act to take their intro applause. Recently there has become a common trend to stop the oncoming act and shake their

hand or even in some cases give them a hug. This has grown mainly because of tv comedy shows and high level acts introducing each other.

This to me is not a good move, it slows the show, stops the act from making a clean start and distracts from their entrance.

The way I introduce an act is to:

Announce the name of the act and extend my arm, (the one not holding the microphone) towards the oncoming act. If the act is coming on stage right I will have the microphone in my left hand and vise versa as required. As the act walks on stage I drop my extended arm and still smiling I walk backwards towards my exit point.

If the act is walking on from stage right, I will exit stage left, and of course vice versa if they are coming on from stage left.

I will time my exit so that I am completely off stage before the act hits their mark, so I am totally out of sight before the introduction applause has finished.

Whilst the act is on:
The act is on stage and you have the length of the act to go backstage or stand at the side until it is your time to come back on and bring the act off and introduce the next act.

So what do you do whilst the act is on?

Stay nearby:
You never know when you will be needed back onstage, if something happens you need to be ready to step up and take over.

- I have had acts walk off stage. This is a rare occurrence, it does happen but mostly with very new acts who panic or have a mental block. The other main reason is because the act has been heckled and decides to exit the stage rather than interact.

- I have had acts booed off, this is very rare, but sometimes an act will do something or say something and it creates a negative reaction with the crowd.

- There could be an emergency situation. This could lead to a temporary stopping of the show and maybe even a complete evacuation of the room.

No matter what the reason, you need to be ready to stand up and retake control, this is especially true if the act has been booed off. The audience is now in a negative slump and you need to bring them back up and carry on with the show.

Be professional:
Standing at the side of the stage checking your facebook or messing around with the other acts is not only unprofessional but it also undermines the act that is on stage.

You are basically saying to the audience that you have no interest in the act and this will subconsciously convey to the audience that they do not need to be interested in the act either.

Patience is a virtue:
Most acts will have a closing up section, where they will thank the audience, any volunteers, the stage staff ect.

This is also a subtle cue for you to be ready to bring them off and back on for a bow if that is in the nature of the show.

If they do not have this section, maybe they are a silent act or a musical act, then you have the previously mentioned compere sheet or compere notes so you know what their last item is and thus know when to bring them off.

During this closing section of the act DO NOT hover at the side of the stage with an eager look to get back on, let the act finish in their own time without distracting the audience.

Bringing the act off:
When the act finishes you can walk onto the stage and bring the act out for a final bow. Bringing the act off is as important as bringing the act on and follows some of the same rules.

- Wait for the act to actually finish before you start to speak.
  A good act will have a natural closing moment that is an applause cue, allow them to reach it and get their applause before you bring them off.

  If you do not know the end of the set and you announce too soon you could essentially ruin the end of the act for both the performer and the audience.

- When you bring the act off, leave their name till the very end in the same way as when you bring the act on.

  "Ladies and gentleman, please keep that applause going and welcome back to take their final bow, the one, the only ...
  ... Mr Wayne Goodman."

- Do not speak whilst the act is taking a bow, allow them to have the moment. You may speak whilst they walk out, and whilst they walk off but only talk about the act that is on.

An example of this would be:

"Ladies and gentlemen, please welcome back on stage to take a bow, the one and only Mr Wayne Goodman"

Pause whilst the act takes their bow, allow them to have the applause.

As the act leaves the stage:

"One more time, Mr … Wayne Goodman"

- Allow the act to get all the way off the stage before you bring the applause to an end and start your introduction for the next act.

- If the act garners a huge round of applause and / or a standing ovation, allow the act to take the bow and leave and maybe come back on for a second bow to show appreciation to the audience.

Chapter Ten

The tools at your disposal.

Every compere, host and emcee is different.
We all have our own individual skill sets and personalities and we should use them to maximise our impact with the audience.

It is natural when you think about a compere to think of a comedian on stage just filling the time with joke after joke, however not every compere has to be funny, and you need to look at what your skill set is, to decide what tools you are going to use.

Using comedy:
As a compere, comedy is a perfect partner, and if you are funny or have the ability to be funny then using comedy and writing a funny script for the show should pose no problem.

If you are planning on using comedy for your script you need to consider a few points.

Try to avoid in-jokes.
In-jokes can be funny, but they do alienate any members of the audience who are not IN on the joke.

I have seen comperes make a joke or comment about a situation that happened backstage that meant nothing to the audience, instead it created a lull moment that just did not fit with the rest of the presentation.

There are exceptions to this rule, if for instance you are at a convention and during one of the presentations something happens that everyone witnesses, then a call back to this in the evening show, or the awards ceremony will be a great addition.

Write and rehearse.
Once you have decided to use some comedy in your role as compere, then you need to make sure it fits your personality and make sure you can tell it properly and it is in fact … funny.

Write your script and then rehearse it, as much as you can. If you find that certain jokes do not feel right when you say it, then drop it. You may also find that whilst you rehearse you actually think of other jokes you can add to the script thus enhancing what you have already written.

Using music:
A compere should always have a play on and play off, (music that is played as you walk on at the beginning and walk off at the end), and also music to introduce your acts/speakers.

I have seen some compere's use music to create jokes, tell stories or just sing a song between acts, all these are a great way to add a little variety to the evening.

When I was 24 I worked on a great ship called the "Dana Anglia" which sailed between Esbjerg, Denmark and Harwich, England. At 10pm every evening we performed a show for the passengers which included my one hour cabaret magic show and the entertainments manager would be host and compere and do a spot too.

I was lucky enough to work with two great entertainment managers, Paul C and Andrew F.

Paul C was amazing, very funny and would tell a few jokes and stories and sing some great songs for the audience.

Andrew was also brilliant and would sing and play a trumpet for his set. The trumpet really made his act stand out from the other ents managers because it was a small room and the audience was not prepared for just how loud a trumpet can be.

When it became time to introduce me he would announce that he was going to play my intro music for me and as he reached for the trumpet, he would actually grab an old style on-the-hob kettle and play the kettle to bring me on.

It did not take me long to appreciate that I was actually sharing my intro with Andrew's ending and rather than just nice round of applause I was actually walking on stage to a huge ovation.

I always think about this as if I was walking out of the sea onto a beach, a small wave on the back of the legs may propel me forwards but a huge wave is going to carry me far up the beach.

That is how this introduction would affect my show, the huge applause would allow me to open my show with a harder impact and that applause would carry me through my opening effect.

The pressure is now on me to maintain the momentum.

I do not have a picture of the actual kettle but it was very similar to this one.

My main point of this story is to highlight that you do not need to follow the normal routes of the compere, be yourself and use the tools you have to create a greater impact not only for your presence but also for the acts / speakers too.

Using magic:
I understand that although I am a magician, and I am writing this book for magicians, that not all readers will in fact be magicians.

However just because you do not do magic, does not mean you should skip this section as there are some amazing routines that you can use to great effect.

Using magic as a compere can be great but you have to remember that you are not the act, you are the glue that holds the acts together so do not use anything that upstages the acts or drags out the running or the speed of the show.

If you have prepared properly then you should know how long you have between each act and create the spaces properly.

Compere tricks:
Believe it or not, there are some magic tricks that are referred to as compere tricks.

Now admittedly these are more pseudo magic rather than actual magic tricks, but do not let that diminish the effect they can have.

The barcode:
This is a classic compere gag trick.
The magician / compere shows an envelope and explains there is a prediction inside.

A spectator names a supermarket, then chooses an everyday item to buy from the selected supermarket and decides on a price for the chosen item.

Let's say the spectator chooses: **Tesco's - Banana's - £1**

The compere now opens the envelope and asks,

"If I have Tesco's Bananas for £1 on this prediction, would that be amazing?"

Of course the spectator says "yes", and so the compere turns the card around to show a barcode from a supermarket.

What is great about this, is you can make it last a minute or five minutes, depending on your personality and how long you want to milk the joke.

I have used the barcode many times, also I have used pieces from my own act to fill the bridge time between acts.

If you are going to use magic as the compere as part of a larger magic show then you must remember that you are the compere and not a stand alone act.

The one rule of being a compere you do not want to break is:

"Never upstage or try to upstage the acts".

The job of the compere is to complement not compete with the acts.

Running Gags / Tricks.
Some comperes will employ the use of a running joke or a running trick, this is a trick or joke that repeats throughout the show.

A great running gag / trick I saw in one show, and it really caused a laugh throughout the show, was the classic magic trick the lota vase.

The Lota vase is an old magic trick, water is poured from vase or bowl until it is empty. Later, more water is poured from the same vase. This can be repeated several times during the show, yet the vase remains in full view of the audience the entire time!

The compere had made or obtained a lota vase that looked like a simple water jug and everytime he walked on stage he completely filled a glass with water, showed the jug was empty and had a drink. The first time this not really noticed as anything special, by the third time he filled the glass it was getting a laugh and by the end of the show, it was anticipated and more confusing for the audience who would laugh, cheer and clap louder every time.

Another idea for a running gag that I did years ago when working in Benidorm for a hotel chain as in house entertainment was that I was going to perform a classic of magic. I informed the audience I would perform the classic torn and restored newspaper.

I showed a newspaper and opened it up and tore down the middle of the paper, then I tore it again, and again, each time tearing down the middle until I was holding a lot of torn newspaper.

I then announced I would restore the paper, but at that moment I was stopped by another entertainer who told me the act was ready and waiting to come on, I apologised to the audience, said we would finish up later and brought the act on.

After the act had finished I returned to the stage and informed the audience I would instead find a chosen card lost in a pack. I had a card selected and lost in the pack, the cards were returned to me and I removed one card. I was just about to reveal the card when once again I was informed the next act was ready to start. I put the card back in the pack, again informed the audience I would finish it later and introduced the next act. This continued with every bridge in the show until the very end of the show, by this time the audience was in on the joke and laughing each time I was stopped at the crucial moment.

At the end of the show I said I would cut and restore a piece of rope, I cut the rope in half and at the moment I was about to restore it, I stopped, looked off stage and when no one stopped me, I called the other entertainer and asked why he had not stopped me, he said there was no more acts and I could finish the show. I looked at the cut rope, then the audience, then the rope again and looking sheepish, I tell the audience I had been expecting the trick to be stopped, this brought more laughter to the crowd and then applause as I restore the rope and take my bow.

A good running gag is worth its weight in gold, but also it can distract from the show, so you need to use it at the right time in the right show.

I used this routine in the hotel I was based in, the guests new my personality, knew I was a good magician and so I used that against them and actually went the opposite direction and it worked for me in that instance. If I was in a show where I was unknown, with acts that were also not regulars in the venue I would avoid this kind of routine.

Chapter Eleven

The Headliner

The headliner is the main act, the famous comedian or the keynote speaker.

The headline act is the last one on the bill, in some ways the whole show is a build up to them coming on.

In other words, they are the star of the show.

This does not mean that you need to treat them any differently, all acts should be dealt with in the same way, with the same respect.

Speak to the headliner as you would the other acts and make sure you know exactly how they would like to be introduced and brought off.

The headliner may have a few concerns or conditions that will need to be addressed and implemented.

I once had a magic act tell me to read his introduction word for word or they would not come on.

There was to be 100% no deviation from the scripted introduction.

After the show, I chatted to the act backstage and he told me that he had in the past had some really bad comperes, so now he does not take the risk and demands his own introduction.

Encore and extended applause:
The headline act will often if not always have a false tab, or encore.
You will need to speak to the act to ensure you know exactly when to bring them off and back on again.

If the headliner is a major name or celebrity then you will also have to contend with extended applause and maybe multiple call backs.

In 2015 I worked with a top end headliner at a university summer ball, he was a regular on top tv shows like "Mock the week" and "live at the Apollo". Before the show I was invited into his dressing room and we had a chat about what he wanted and how he wanted it.

He was lovely and so easy to work with, but he warned me he would probably make 3 or 4 applause comebacks.

This was no problem and because we had chatted about how he wanted to do it, I was able to accommodate it easily and make it happen for him.

Chapter Twelve

Closing the show

The acts have all done their part, the headliner or keynote speaker has delivered their act or speech and now it is time to close the show.

I have seen many comperes in the past ruin the end of the show because they think the job is done so they let the energy levels drop, this is a huge mistake.

Your headliner has completed their act and the audience is at their peak, now is the time to cash it all in and bring the show to an end with as much energy as possible.

Keep the applause going:
This is so important and so easy to accomplish.
You need to thank the staff and acts so do this with some more applause.

- Thank the sound and light technicians.
- Thank the backstage team.
- Thank the venue and bar staff.
- Thank all the individual acts.
- Thank the headliner.
- Thank the audience.

Some shows have had all the acts ready to come back on and take a bow when they are called, this is great when it happens as you end up with the whole stage full of people, all waving and bowing as the audience all clap and cheer louder and louder for each act that returns to the stage.

Do not forget yourself:
You are also a major part of the show and you should also ask for a round of applause for yourself.

I have seen acts directly ask for a round of applause for themselves but I find this a little self indulgent. I would rather ask in a non direct manner.

I would not say:

"And finally, let's have a round of applause for your compere … Me"

I am not a fan, if this works for your personality and the style of the show then great, but it is not for me.

I would say:

"And finally, thank you all so much for being an amazing audience, from everyone here, the staff, the acts and of course from myself, thank you and goodnight".

It is a natural applause cue, I have already named all the individual acts and staff teams, but for the final moment I put them all together and myself and thank the audience as I take my bow.

Job done.

Off stage messages:
Sometimes you will be asked to deliver a message to the audience at the end of the show.

This may include a line up for the next show, or an important message about the next days events or an after show party.
I will always insist that these messages are delivered off stage after the final applause. This prevents the messages becoming a low point and killing the end of the show.

I will leave the stage, the applause still going. I will head off stage and wait for 5 - 10 seconds before announcing something along the lines of:

"Thank you once again ladies and gentlemen for attending tonight's show, we would like to remind you all that the after show party will begin in 15 minutes in the main bar area"

This delivers the message as everyone is about to stand and leave the venue but does not diminish the ending of the show.

A Chat with Sheriton Swan.

Sheriton Swan is a full time theatre technician, I have worked with Sheriton many times over the years at magic conventions and theatre shows as both an act and also as a compere.

When I started this book I knew his knowledge would be essential and he was kind enough to answer any questions I sent him.

As well as the general technical details I required to complete certain chapters, Sheriton was also kind enough to answer a few general questions I put to him.

Why is a light and sound check important for an emcee/compere?
The compere is often the first person that the audience see and hear; they're also on the stage more often than any of the acts.

Ensuring that everything technical is sorted and working for every act, and that does include the compere, makes for a much better show. It's not a very slick start to the show if you walk out in a blackout, accompanied by a squeal of feedback!

The crew will often be at their busiest prepping for the next act whilst you're on stage so if your requirements are already sorted out before your first entrance, it'll help the show to move along more smoothly.

What questions would you ask the compere and what questions would you expect to be asked by the compere?
The crew need to know each time that you'll be on stage and also if you'll be making any off-stage announcements. Microphones won't routinely be left live and most sound engineers won't be keen on performers switching them on/off themselves.

Any sound or lighting cues will also need to be explained and possibly rehearsed.

If you're working with a followspot, they'll need to know from which side of stage you'll be entering each time.

If you have any requirements that are in any way out of the ordinary, it's always prudent to give advance notice to the organisers / venue.

It's often expected that the compere's requirements will be very simple so if you need anything special, get in touch before the day of the show.

Do you have any stories about nightmare comperes?
I recall one compere who insisted on using his own (very cheap) radio mic. The venue had much better equipment available but he wouldn't budge and during the show it sounded awful and kept cutting out; it made him look bad and the show suffered as a result. Moral of the story listen to the crew, they know more about technical theatre than you do.

It's a particular pet hate of mine when comperes come on after the last act and attempt to speak at length and thank everyone and their dog whilst the audience start trying to leave.

It's a huge anti-climax to the show. Get the parish notices out of the way before the finale and let the show finish on a high.

I have mentioned in the chapter about lighting cues with a red/green system, do you have any other ways of communicating with the compere using the lights and sounds?
In the absence of cue lights, it's not unusual to just dip one of the stage lights in the performers' eye line. This can be done reasonably subtly so it's not too obvious to the audience.

If you're in the middle of a routine with some time still to go, it's useful if you can in some way (subtly) acknowledge that you've seen the signal, eye contact with one of the crew at the back of the stalls and a slight nod is enough.

Without any acknowledgement, the crew may think that you've not noticed the cue and resort to more extreme measures. Jumping up & down, waving hands in the air, flashing torches etc – if the audience ever turn around at the wrong time, they'll sometimes see more going on behind them than on stage!

What is the main role of the lighting and sound engineers?
The technical crew are there to help you present your act in the best possible (metaphorical and literal) light.

There are both technical considerations (can the performer be seen and heard) and artistic considerations (does the performer look good and is the lighting appropriate and supportive, do they sound natural etc).

Crew are almost universally overworked and underpaid so if you bring them a hot beverage, they'll always go the extra mile for you to make the show that little bit better.

Acknowledgements

Thanks to:

Sheriton Swan, for his assistance and input in this book.

Richard Whymark

Simon Shaw, Brian Watson and Elliot Philip's for their pre edit read throughs and assistance, this book would not have been finished without your help.

Michael Murray for his invaluable input and cover art.

Rodney James Piper for his assistance and knowledge.

For more reading on the subject I would highly recommend "Beyond Compere" by Terry Seabrook.

Glossary of terms

Throughout this book you will see some words that apply to the world of theatre and stage work. I have included a glossary of terms for those you may not be familiar with.

AD LIB:
From Latin Ad libitum meaning "at one's pleasure".
To speak or perform with having previously prepared the script or routine.

BACKSTAGE:
The part of the stage unseen to the audience. This could be behind scenery, curtains or under the stage.

BLACKOUT:
A complete absence of stage lighting of any kind

CENTRE STAGE:
The middle portion of the stage - has good sightlines to all seats.

CUE LIGHT:
A system or device that enables cues to be delivered from the technicians to the compere or act on stage.
Normal lighting systems have a red for "Not ready" and green for "Ready" lighting configuration.

CURTAIN CALL:
At the end of a performance, the acknowledgement of applause by either the headline act / keynote speaker or entire cast etc.

DRESS REHEARSAL:
A full rehearsal, with all technical and creative elements brought together. The performance as it will be 'on the night'.

ENCORE:
An extra routine, song or performance required by the demand of the audience. Most acts have a routine or song ready in case of an encore.

ENTRANCE:
The act of the performer walking onto the stage.

FINALE:
the last part of a piece of music, an entertainment, or a public event, especially when particularly dramatic or exciting.

FOLLOW SPOT:
Usually, a powerful single white light, mounted in or above the auditorium, used with an operator so that the light beam can be moved around the stage to follow the performer. Sometimes a beam light or other lantern may be used in the same way.

FRONT OF CURTAINS:
The part of the stage constantly visible to the audience, even when the curtains are closed.

FRONT OF HOUSE:
Every part of the theatre in front of the proscenium arch. Includes foyer areas open to the general public. Also known as FOH.

GREEN ROOM:
A room backstage for the performers in the show to relax and wait for their time on stage.

HOUSE:
Normally refers to the seating and performance area of the venue..

HOUSE LIGHTS:
The house lighting which is commonly faded out when the performance starts.

PRESHOW:
The period before the performance begins.

PROPS:
Items used on stage by the performer for their own act.

REHEARSAL:
To run through the act on stage.
A technical rehearsal is a run through with light and sound technicians required to ensure smooth running of the act.

RUN-THROUGH:
A full or partial rehearsal of the show.

SOUND CHECK:
A thorough test of the sound system before a performance.

STAGE CREW:
Also referred to as backstage crew, these crew members are responsible for moving props and equipment behind the curtain between acts or as the act requires on stage during the performance.

STAGE LEFT / RIGHT:
Left/ Right as seen from the Actor's point of view on stage. (ie Stage Left is the right side of the stage when looking from the auditorium.)
Please note that in some european countries the opposite is employed.

STALLS:
The lowest audience seating area, usually just below the level of the stage, in a proscenium theatre.

STANDING OVATION:
The audience applauds and stands at the same time. Its is seen as a higher level of applause

TABS:
The house curtains.

WINGS:
The area at each side of the stage that is out of view of the audience.

Thank you so much for purchasing and reading this book.
If you would like to read more by the Wayne Goodman please contact:
wayne@waynegoodman.co.uk

Also by Wayne Goodman:
The Comedy Magicians Joke Book vol 1.
The Comedy Magicians Joke Book vol 2.
The Comedy Magicians Joke Book vol 3.
The Complete Comedy Magicians Joke Book.
The Definitive Guide to Restaurant Magic.
The Expert at the Restaurant Table.
Plan, Prepare, Perform.
Go Compere.

Booklets by Wayne Goodman:
The Jedi Principle.
The Lean.
The Restaurant Course.

Tricks by Wayne Goodman:
Lord of the Bling.
Look Sharp.
Prism.
Clone.
Marked.
Sam the bell hog.
Asbo.
Time Traveller.
Royal Brainwave.
WG Comedy Prediction.
421 Card.

By Wayne and Charlee Goodman:
Cook with Charlee.
Amazing jokes for 8 - 10 year olds.

www.ingramcontent.com/pod-product-compliance
Lightning Source LLC
Chambersburg PA
CBHW070741230426
43669CB00014B/2539